To Gil,

Thank You for Letting me be creative You are Like a brother. You Give Great meaning to Family, I Love How You Love Your Family

Love
GG

SPIRITUAL COMPASS

Garry Guerrier

DEDICATION

I dedicate this book to my loving sister Mona, may she rest in perfect peace, my dad, mom, and all of my sisters, Ginette, Danielle, Mirelle, Linda, Nadine, and my brother, Frantz.

I would like to thank my mentor and best friend, Bill, for all his support, love, and wisdom.

It would take so many more pages to honor the people who are special in my life, and who have made a lasting mark, so I will just honor your names: Billy, Dave, Lance, Larry, Shahe, Nicole, Bea, Sean, Greg, Ronnie, Gabe, Anna, Dawn, Heidi, Mae, Dana, Tracy, Ryan, Sandy, Anjelica, Chelsea, Clare, Maryann, Theo, Donna, Jerian, Linda, Gary, Pilar, Danny, Leslie Pam, Julia, Christy, Inger, Lauryn, Veronica, Ezra, Amy, Alex, Roger, Steve, Jane, Shirley, Chisell, Desdanie, Phil, Karen, Aundrea, and my Men's Meeting.

A SPECIAL THANK-YOU TO:

Pete, Nora, Andrew, Leslie, Zack, and Maria; D.W. Jones and Nephi Sicajan for the book cover; and David Weiss for the Introduction.

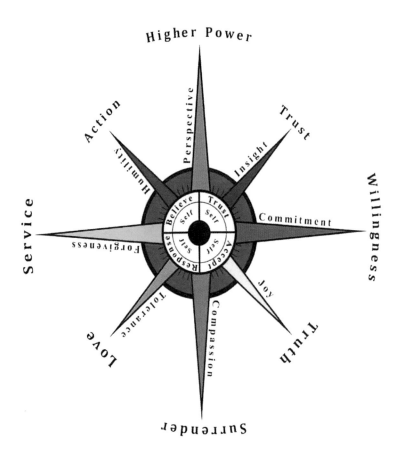

CONTENTS

Prologue..x

Spiritual Compass Introduction 1

Compass Points 4

Identity.. 5

Self-Belief.. 8

Self-Acceptance 10

Self-Responsiveness 13

Self-Trust.. 16

Higher Power 18

Service... 20

Surrender...22

Willingness...24

Truth...26

Love..28

Action... 30

Trust 32

Compassion.. 34

Tolerance 36

Forgiveness... 38

Humility... 40

Perspective..42

Insight 45

Commitment..47

Joy...49

Colors.. 51

Spirituality.. 53

Relationship... 55

People Pleasing 57

Personal Responsibility.. 59

Self-Criticism..62

Control.. 64

Fear.. 66

Environment 69

Social Media..70

Excuses Excuses Excuses...72

Gratitude..74

Fun...76

How To Use The Spiritual Compass................................79

About The Author 95

Glossary 98

Testimonials 101

PROLOGUE

For most of us, there's a handful of phone calls you never forget. The one from my sister, Nadine, about my estranged daughter, Anjelica, is high on my list. Growing up in an all-girl house, a kid needs an ally. Nadine was mine. So it meant a lot that my now -grown daughter had reached out to my favorite sis, especially since neither of us had seen or heard from my "little Angel" since she was 23 -and she'd soon be 27.

Hanging up with Nadine, my mind wandered back to that warm summer day in Buckhead, Georgia, when I last saw my girl. I was nervous but excited about our meeting, after not hearing from Angelica for more than four years. I suggested my friend Greg's restaurant, The Tavern. It had intimate seating and I knew my daughter would love the food. Also, Greg has a daughter Anjelica's age, so he gets it. My little girl - now a young woman - arrived, and we sat.

I don't know why I thought this time would be different, but there was still tension in the air. Angelica was cold and her responses short. I tried to warm the mood by telling her how much I missed her and loved her. But she just looked down at her barely eaten sandwich and closed her eyes.

My divorce from Anjelica's mom had been rough on our girl. Understandably, she felt abandoned and as a result, she started pulling away. It was hard for me not to feel hurt or to try to "rescue her" from the reality of the situation. But I remembered the experience of my friend Nate, who had a similar falling out with his son. Nate was a doer and a fixer. He was used to moving mountains at work and commanded respect for all his achievements. So he was sure he knew how to win back his son. Years on, all that chasing and pleading and attempts to coax, bribe, or threaten his son have only driven them further apart.

On the other hand, my friend Pete - whose daughter had also "disowned" him after his divorce - had charted a different course. His daughter couldn't forgive him for remarrying - and her abuse of alcohol wasn't helping their situation. I was helping Pete with a program of emotional/spiritual recovery (the forerunner to this book), frequently sharing notes and giving him help along the way. As a result, Pete chose to give his daughter the dignity of her own journey. He didn't chase, threaten, bribe, or even reach out, apart from his initial insistence that he loved her and would always be there waiting should she want to return.

Sure enough, after a few years of silence, she texted him. Then a call. And then a coffee. Today, after a slow thaw, they are once again close. I remember thinking at the time - even though I had helped Pete build up the courage to choose his direction - my God, where do you get the strength to… "don't just do something… *stand there!*"

Ironically, now it was my turn to practice what I preached. I walked Anjelica to her car, where I hoped we could finish our conversation, but she insisted on leaving. I asked if there was *anything* I could do to help make things better between us. Her response floored me. She simply said, "No. You are dead to me." Then she closed her door and drove away.

I have served in the Army, crushed my rigorous boot camp, excelled at karate and boxing, volunteered as a New York City firefighter, started a men's meeting where hundreds of brave souls come to be vulnerable and grow. I have personally mentored more than 500 strong and fearless souls, yet here I was, stunned, shot in the heart, by a few simple words from a wounded daughter.

I don't know how long I stood in the parking lot of Greg's restaurant, but when I finally got in my car, I wept like never before. How could I have hurt someone I loved *so much?* On the flight back to Los Angeles I realized it was going to take all the tools I had been preaching, teaching, and mentoring all these years, if I had any chance of gracefully allowing Angelica to choose her own path. I felt lost without her, and a strong impulse to do *anything* to get her back. But if I was going to allow her the dignity of her own journey, I was going to need to find the courage to do so. Sometimes, doing "nothing" is the hardest, bravest of all.

In the ensuing months and years, I journaled and sought the wisdom of my own mentor, support groups, and other outside help. I devoured books and courses on emotional recovery, and spent hours speaking honestly and lovingly to myself in the mirror (literally and figuratively, in the "Mirror Process" — covered later in this book). Slowly, the years of my training, teaching, mentoring, began to solidify into the pages you are about to read - a Spiritual Compass - grounded in the "north pole" of a Higher Power and the qualities of perspective, humility, and forgiveness.

Utilizing the tools that I have assembled for you here, in an organized directional guide to spiritual maturity and strength, I was able to give my daughter the dignity to experience her feelings and let go of my vise grip on control. The phone call I mentioned above came just a few months ago, as I was completing this book. Nadine had called to say Angelica had reached out to her. First a simple text, to say hello. Then a call. More recently, they've had a few wonderful visits. And, though Angelica hasn't reached out to me directly, she asks about me. Do I want to rush in and "speed the thaw"? You bet I do. And, as we will discuss in later chapters, these feelings are valid. All feelings "have a seat in the car." They just don't get to drive. If I rush in now, I risk pushing Angelica away again, as Nate did his son. But, by setting my course by my spiritual compass, I can find the strength, insight, and courage to make better choices.

You don't have to have a daughter to know we all face tremendous emotional and spiritual challenges in our lives. Perhaps you're struggling with a lonely single life. Maybe you're in a difficult relationship or going through a painful breakup or divorce. Do you have stress at a difficult job? Or worse, perhaps you're facing unemployment, underemployment, or chronic pain or illness.

Whatever our challenge, we mustn't let our *feelings* set the course of our life. For that we need a spiritual compass. I wrote this book to share the experience, strength, and knowledge that I have gained over the years, that have given me the strength to let go of my vise grip and trust in my Higher Power. In my case it's allowed my daughter to slowly come back into my family, as just one of many personal, emotional, and spiritual victories, large and small.

I invite you to make this book your own. I am confident that if you apply the principles in these pages, you will discover a new perspective. You will be able to look into the Compass, change the direction of your life, and reach the destination your Higher Power has for you. Join me on the journey, won't you?

In gratitude,
Garry G

SPIRITUAL COMPASS INTRODUCTION

A compass is a navigational instrument that is powered by the magnetic force of the earth, which shows directions when you are lost, and helps you find your way. The Spiritual Compass reminds you that, though we live in a world of hurry, worry, distractions, problems, and judgment, at every turn we can gain a new perspective and redirect our focus. With this practice of the Spiritual Compass, we put ourselves back on track to harmony and inner peace, creating new coping skills for everyday life. This is not about "positive thinking." If you get lost in the wilderness without a compass to help you get to where you need to be, it doesn't matter how positive your thinking is, you're still going to be lost. Thinking positively will only let you be happy about being lost. You need guidance in order to get back, to get back to your own power.

The different points on the Spiritual Compass are: Identity, Self-Belief, Self-Acceptance, Self-Responsiveness, Self-Trust, Higher Power, Service, Surrender, Willingness, Truth, Love, Action, Trust, Compassion, Tolerance, Forgiveness, Humility, Perspective, Insight, Commitment, and Joy.

The Spiritual Compass will guide you and give you exactly what you need at this moment. At times, all you need is a little perspective. You already have the willingness or you wouldn't be reading this book.

The spiritual journey is not a destination; it is evolving from one level to the next, often repeating similar experiences with new and different perspectives. It's your blueprint. I believe that everyone is born with a blueprint. Each blueprint intertwines with other blueprints that cross your path. For example, my sister Mona died at a young age from cancer, and her blueprint was to learn how to combat the cancer and die young. Part of my family's blueprints and mine was to have my sister die young, and to learn from the different aspects of this experience. My sister's husband's blueprint was to deal with a dying wife. You fulfill your blueprint in life and, in turn, you complete the blueprint of others. Hence, the quote "People come into your life for a reason, season, or a lifetime," which means that we meet people who will guide us, teach us, or walk along the same path together with us.

Whether you find yourself on your spiritual path at this moment or not, this is exactly where you need to be. The universe is a dynamic place where the energies are constantly changing and shifting. Obtaining this Spiritual Compass and reading this one page allows you to see that we are all connected through our energy. If you are unhappy with your situation, you have lessons to learn from it. No situation is ever permanent.

No matter how difficult your lesson is, you have to believe in the process, and you must trust and take the leap of faith.

No one person is better or more accomplished spiritually than another, as each of us is on our own unique path. Each path is full of lessons that have been created by our soul in order to accomplish its purposes in our lifetime. Each of your lessons has been created with the knowledge that you would use your spiritual guidance to resolve it. At times, you may be led to others to help you, or it is part of their spiritual journey to help you with yours.

Your journey may seem long and difficult, but with this Spiritual Compass, it is merely the way in which your soul reconnects you with your power and also brings your spiritual nature into prominence. Remember that you are, and have always been, all-knowing and all-powerful. Trust the Spiritual Compass and you will move forward on your path with greater ease.

The Spiritual Compass is user friendly. Thoughts and feelings have their own magnetic energy that attracts energy of a similar nature. First, you'll want to center yourself by breathing. Take the time to look at the Spiritual Compass. Whatever evokes or triggers an emotion is exactly what you need at that moment. Turn to the corresponding section in this book to read a new perspective. I find it extremely helpful to keep a journal, where I write down what I am feeling.

COMPASS POINTS

1. Identity

2. Self-Belief

3. Self-Acceptance

4. Self-Responsiveness

5. Self-Trust

6. Higher Power

7. Service

8. Surrender

9. Willingness

10. Truth

11. Love

12. Action

13. Trust

14. Compassion

15. Tolerance

16. Forgiveness

17. Humility

18. Perspective

19. Insight

20. Commitment

21. Joy

IDENTITY

Your identity began when your parents came together to connect their chromosomes, forming an embryonic cell with your unique DNA. That cell forms millions of cells that separate and multiply, becoming your brain, spine, and each individual organ's cells. None of the millions of people who came before you, who are living now, and who will come after you, will have cells identical to yours, unless you have a twin from the same egg. We forget just how powerful and unique we are. No one is like you. Once you understand that, you can begin to grow into your own power with the power that is already in you.

The second part of your identity is what you have collected in your clean pure sponge. I use the analogy of a sponge because it absorbs. You are born simple, fresh, and pure, what I like to call SFP. When you are a child, you begin collecting in your sponge whatever you are taught or brainwashed or conditioned to say, do, and believe. It makes me extremely sad when I see little white-supremacy kids screaming "nigger" or little Muslim kids screaming and hating Jewish people. I was reading the newspaper (yes, I am one of the few left who actually like to read a paper). It was an article about two Irish men who shot each other because one was a Protestant and the other Catholic. Neither even went to church. When we really examine our fears, worries, or doubts about something, we sometimes notice that they are not based on our own experience. Often, if we trace our fear, worry, and doubt back to its source, we find that one of our parents may have handed it down to us. Our mother or father may have had an intense fear, worry, or doubt, stemming from his or her own life experiences. If that fear was not resolved by the time you were born, chances are that it was passed down to you. Meanwhile, you may have no actual corresponding experiences, so being fearful doesn't make any sense, and it may even block you from doing things you want to do.

Keeping in mind that your parents were only using the tools they had, and that most of their errors in judgment were made with the best intentions, it might be time to release these fears symbolically. A good method I use is to write everything down on a piece of paper, light it on fire, and then burn it up completely. You can use whatever is symbolic to you. Note that you cannot resolve others' fears for them, but you can decide to let go of your own, whether your parents are still alive or not. The more we do this deep inner work with our fears, worries, and doubts, the better we will be able to parent ourselves and our children. Either way, the effect will be to weaken the chance of passing them on. It's important to remember that it's never too late. If you don't work on them, you will continue to believe that they are your truth or identity, and you will go through life defending them. Hopefully, one day, as you go through the journey of life and search for your own, true identity, you will have an awakening, when you can begin to collect truth and good things in your sponge, maybe even one with a scrubby side, to keep all negativity out.

Identity plays a large and significant role in shaping each of our lives, such as personality attributes and knowledge of one's skills and abilities. For example, the statement "I am lazy" is a self-assessment that contributes to the self-concept, but, in contrast, the statement

"I am tired" would not be considered part of someone's self-concept, since being tired is a temporary state. This awareness of one's unique identity - "Who am I?"- is a question everyone at some point asks himself or herself. Believing that the answer will come from studying philosophies developed in the Stone Age, or consulting a guru, are not practical ways to understand or change who you are. We need to seek and find our true identity by examining who we are, and more importantly, creating who we want to be. This will help the way you look at yourself and your relationship to the world. It's a journey, not a destination, and it allows you the opportunity to grow continuously.

SELF-BELIEF

Self-belief is essential to the core of who you are. It becomes the foundation of personal development, giving you the confidence to fulfill the immeasurable potential of all that was, is, and will be.

One of my clients wanted to skip his turn to lead a meeting via teleconference because he had never done it before. He called and asked if he should pass his turn to his co-host. I informed him he had the ability not only to lead the meeting but to thrive, and if he chose not to because of fear, he would miss the opportunity to learn, grow, and build his self-belief.

We can do many things in our lives. If we embrace the concept of self-belief to enhance our abilities, we can overcome the fear, worry, and doubt that infuse our lives and that we have adapted to through conditioning. My mom, bless her heart, is one of the most loving people I know, but she has a chaotic way of expressing her worries and fears. When we get on elevators, any little jolt she feels, she immediately goes into panic mode, holding onto the walls, and screaming, "Oh my God, what's going on?" For me, as a little kid, it was scary. It wasn't until I was older that I could walk into an elevator and know I would be safe. I had to build my self-belief and confidence. The necessary thing is having the desire to put aside all those outer influences and thoughts, then to go inward to your core to see the magnificent self. In doing so, you will conquer those barriers and obstacles. You'll begin to see this magic in its truest and highest form. Having fear, worry, and doubt will only attract more of the same predicament. Let us celebrate what we do have, and know that with belief and determination, we can make every day splendid and blissful. We no longer have to feel empty, hollow, or lacking. We can look in the mirror knowing that we are living and have lived the best life possible. Life is not about reaching a destination in pure, clean condition, unharmed and without scars. Out of pain and suffering, you gain strength. Though many of us have suffered and struggled, it is important to realize that this is a part of life. Know that everything you've experienced in your life has made you who you are. Believe in yourself. Know that your mind, body, and spirit have all merged into one powerful being called you.

Positive Self-Belief

List 10 positive things about yourself. If you can't think of 10, write down as many as you can; then come back and add more as you grow.

1. _____
2. _____
3. _____
4. _____
5. _____
6. _____
7. _____
8. _____
9. _____
10. _____

SELF-ACCEPTANCE

Self-acceptance is accepting yourself as you are and knowing that it is the way you were created. We all start with our blueprint (an original plan or a prototype). I often laugh when I hear the response to the question, "If I could change anything about myself, what would it be?" My nose, my eyes, bigger breasts, bigger butt, blond hair, brunette hair, etc. These are all external changes, whereas love and acceptance come from within. Accepting yourself empowers you. People will accept you the way you accept yourself. If you are negative, people will view you as being negative. If you are happy, positive, and self-loving, people will view you that way. If they don't, it is none of your concern. You can't force anyone to be happy and positive; it has to do with their accepting who they are and loving who they are.

"People are as happy as they choose to be."
–SPIRITUAL COMPASS

Self-acceptance is coming to terms with the fact that you are unique and powerful. Your blueprint is perfect, but what we do is sabotage the beauty by beating ourselves up, by overeating, drinking to excess, doing drugs, having unnecessary plastic surgery, and other harmful behaviors. In the end, we are still unhappy. Until you accept who you are, and see how wonderful that is, you'll still be unhappy. It is true that being your own best friend or loving yourself can be one of the hardest things in life to do, but when accomplished, it is extremely powerful.

Self-acceptance was hard for me. I based my self-acceptance on the approval of others and what I did for them, as opposed to who I was. Seeking validations and acceptance is never successful; it is a road to nowhere. My road to self-friendship began with self-forgiveness. It proceeded to self-acceptance, and it ended with self-celebration. In the end, self-acceptance is a state of being that radiates people's total «okay-ness" with the way they are. It is a complete and positive embracing of their present physical, mental, and spiritual condition. It is absolute self-acceptance. We live in a world where, at every turn, you are pressured to believe that you should be a certain size, wear certain clothes, have a certain kind of hair, house, car, etc., which promotes acceptance in the world. None of that will matter to you when you have self-acceptance. You will be glad not to conform and will begin marching to your own drumbeat. I am not saying you can't have things you like or are passionate about, but those things just won't define who you are.

Ten Signs of Self-Acceptance

1. Self-accepting people are happy people.
2. Self-accepting people are empowered to be their real selves.
3. Self-accepting people have the ability to attend to their own needs.
4. Self-accepting people are in good contact with reality.
5. Self-accepting people are able to laugh at themselves.
6. Self-accepting people beat themselves with a feather, not a bat.

7. Self-accepting people are open to being loved for who they are.

8. Self-accepting people are assertive.

9. Self-accepting people respect their own boundaries.

10. Self-accepting people choose how they will respond instead of automatically reacting.

Don't Judge your self worth by your net worth.
-SPIRITUAL COMPASS

SELF-RESPONSIVENESS

Self-responsiveness is listening to your inner self-your mind, body, and spirit-and responding to it in a gentle and caring way. Our bodies speak to us when we are tired, when we are hungry, when we need to sleep, when we need solitude, serenity, etc. If you possess self-responsiveness, you will respond and take care of what your body, mind, and spirit are asking for. Most people don't respond to this internal communication with self. They keep ignoring the inner voice, which in turn hurts them in the long run. After my lectures, many people have questions and ask for help. "What is wrong with me? I feel tired and depressed." I often respond with, "Listen to your inner self; the answer is always there." Your body is not only unique in how it is built, it is also the best guide to inform you of the remedy to heal it. It is important to listen to yourself.

- I sleep when I'm tired.
- I wake up when I've rested.
- I eat when I'm hungry.
- I withdraw when I'm feeling the need for solitude.
- I make music when my own song bubbles up to the surface.
- I weep when I'm sad.
- I journal when I need serenity for my soul.

You get where I am going. You are the guide and the gauge of your self-responsiveness. Open yourself to listening. I was at an energy class, and in my mind and gut I had the feeling that I forgot to lock my car. "Why all of a sudden?" I asked myself. So I went to my car and, lo and behold, it was unlocked. Normally, in the past, I would have ignored my intuition, but I responded.

It is so important to listen to your gut. It has been with you since you were born, and it has the ability to sense things, like when we see a red flag at the start of a friendship or relationship. Do not ignore these signs in front of you and complain about them later. Egotistically, we feel we have the ability to change a person. When this backfires, we begin to blame or complain. We must realize we are the common denominator of all our dramas. Be diligent in listening in order have the proper response to yourself.

Self-Response Chart

Disgusted

Serenity

Dissapointed

Grateful

Anxious

Bored

Cold

Hot

Self Love

Thoughtful

Confident

Lonely

Exhausted

Hysterical

Happy

Satisfied

SELF-TRUST

This is the reliance on one's own integrity, strength, and ability. When it comes to self-trust, so many of us would rather rely on self-doubt. Did I do this right? Did I do that wrong? Full of doubt, doubt, and more doubt. With self-trust, you are going to have to trust your intuitions and abilities with all your inner strength, not comparing yourself to others or what they do. You can admire someone or what he or she does, but you also have the ability to do what you do in your own powerful and unique way. Building a positive inner dialogue will strengthen your inner authority and serve as an internal orientation toward the outer world. It also allows us to consciously manage collective and inter-generational influences that would otherwise seize our capacity to make soul-directed decisions.

The universe will issue us tasks at different points in our lives, tasks that will challenge us to become more of what we really are. This often involves trials and tribulations of some kind, which requires our authentic self to step up to the plate. The person you need to trust first is yourself. No one can be as consistently supportive of you as you can learn to be. Being kind to yourself increases self-confidence, and it lessens your need for approval. Loving and caring for yourself not only increases self-trust, it also deepens your connection with others. Self-trust means that you can take care of your needs and safety. It means trusting yourself in any situation, and practicing kindness toward yourself, and refusing to give up on yourself. No one is perfect.

The heartbeat of every significant relationship is trust but its foundation is your self-trust. A healthy self-trust is like having an internal GPS system, knowing where to go next, and trusting your decisions, both big and small. You may make mistakes, but you won't fear them. You will no longer suffer from self-doubt, crippling indecision, and the fear of failure. When you seek validation, happiness, approval, or reassurance from someone else, these feelings are short-lived. Instead of trusting the judgment of others, trust your own.

When you trust yourself, you will *love* yourself. We shouldn't make loving ourselves dependent on external factors. You are worthy because you exist. Your self-doubt and perfectionism may be standing in the way of manifesting those gifts, but even if self-doubt is there, let it flow out like a river, finding its way out of your world.

Well-being hinges on self-trust. Is it possible to learn how to trust yourself when you've avoided it your entire life? Of course, since self-trust is your birthright, it was yours from the start and will live inside you, sitting unbroken, until your last breath on this earth. Healing requires commitment, patience, and time. Change doesn't occur in a few days or simple steps. First thing in the morning, instead of reaching for your phone, Instagram, Facebook, Twitter, or any social media, pause and read something inspirational; take a moment for yourself; try to engage in a simple breathing practice.

HIGHER POWER

This is any aspect of belief that can provide an in-depth experience of spiritual consciousness. I had a very religious mother, who tried different religions, like Catholic and Jehovah's Witnesses, ending up Lutheran. Like her, although I went to a Catholic school, I was always eager to research and know more about religions, God, and a higher power. I have in my library the Qur'an, the Bible, the Torah, and the Book of Mormon, amongst many religious books. I have these in order to have compassion for the religious believers I often encounter. I also wanted to research things for myself. I feel that people who want answers should search for the answers themselves instead of allowing others to do the work for them. After all, seek and you shall find, right? My many spiritual trips to far-off places, and the many books I have read, have led me to believe that there is a higher power, name it God, Buddha, Hashem, Lord, Omnipresent, or however you understand it. At their core, they all equate to love, fate, and an aspect of our own consciousness. Higher power allows us the ability to trust in something bigger than ourselves, which can bring serenity to our lives and also lead us to spirituality. Believing in a higher power means that you allow yourself the option of going beyond the sensory world, where a whole new vista opens. With that in mind, we can't allow people to use religion to create fear and to control this world. Instead, for those of us who search for more spiritual depth and balance, we can embark on our own journey of fulfillment. It is powerful to surrender and trust in your higher power.

This spiritual freedom enables you to find a personal understanding of a God of your understanding, and to allow others that freedom as well. As your concept of your Higher power evolves, you continue to change and grow.

The other part of Higher power is you. You were created in the image of the God of your understanding; therefore, you are your own source of higher power as well. The pure bliss of creativity is available to all of us. Higher power doesn't give us the tables, chairs, cabinets, etc.; it just gives us the wood to build with. Don't be afraid to tap into your power. Your higher consciousness is what is inside you, allowing you the ability to believe that everything will be according to what is.

I recommend the following exercise. In the morning, practice something that will reinforce and illuminate your inner trust. Engage in a simple breathing technique: Breathe in self-trust, breathe out self-doubt, trusting that you are enough.

> FAITH AND HOPE is being open-minded
> to the possibilities. We don't have to believe
> something will happen, only that it could.
> -SPIRITUAL COMPASS

SERVICE

Service is giving your time and energy to improve the life of someone else. Many people give to others with the expectation of something in return, which diminishes the dignity and value of our giving. Examples of this would be letting someone go ahead of you in traffic but expecting him to say thank you or respond with a nod; helping a friend to move but expecting her to help you move. Your anger when someone isn't appreciative diminishes the kind act. The remarkable thing about service and giving is that when you do it with love and pure energy, the universe returns it to you in abundance, keeping the flow of the powerful circulation of energy. Through service to others, you also serve your own spiritual development. By loving and healing someone through the use of spiritual energy, you help the spiritually blind to see the light within; you also help the spiritually deaf to hear the whisperings of their souls. The details of how that process unfolds are unique for every individual. We all tread this path in our own way to reach the common goal of reconnecting with the spiritual flame that shines within our hearts. The spiritual being knows that living purposefully involves serving in a loving fashion. Mother Teresa, who spent many years of her life caring for the most downtrodden among us, in the slums of Calcutta, defined purpose this way: "The fruit of love is service." This beautiful world that we live in can only get better when we do our part in service. It can be as small as a hello and a smile, because you never know what an individual may be going through, and that one gesture could be the very thing that makes or saves her day. I truly believe that. We are all capable of making this world a better place together.

I volunteer once a week to feed the homeless at the Midnight Mission. As I was walking around the neighborhood, I saw a hair salon and barbershop. I said hello to the hairdresser and later found out that she had been working there once a week for twenty years for free. I had joy in my heart to know that good people still exist. Instead of asking what life is giving us, perhaps we might profit more by asking what we ourselves can give. By reaching out to help others in a healthy way, we move beyond our problems, and we learn to give unconditionally. Every moment can be an opportunity to be of service and a chance to enhance our lives. Service can show kids and teens that giving their time, effort, and kindness is more rewarding than receiving. It's a powerful example that adults can show children, establishing a foundation that will endure.

SURRENDER

Believing in a power greater than yourself will help relieve you and your ego from being controlled by people, places, events, or things.

We grow up in a society that trains us never to surrender or give up, to fight. Did you ever fight for something so hard, and in the end, you realized it was the very thing you didn't want? Many of us view this as defeat, but in actuality it's the greatest awareness possible. It is natural to want a quick fix or an immediate solution to our problems or situations. As humans, we can dwell on things or have mind chatter, which causes upset and also makes it hard to go about our day or even to sleep. The strong human will often get us in trouble. We aim for many goals, but even when we achieve or acquire them, we are rarely satisfied. They don't make our lives complete, so we create bigger goals and push even harder. Often, if we don't get what we want, we can begin to feel inadequate or deprived. Learning to let go of our will and to surrender will help us acknowledge our powerlessness and can bring serenity. Our culture rushes people through life, work, and relationships. We don't allow ourselves time to let things happen at their own pace. Surrender to the flow of life; take time to go outside and focus on a cloud; watch the leaves on the trees and notice their movement with the breeze. Let the air rush around you and clear your mind. Drink a glass of water or take a relaxing shower to cleanse the negativity from your system. These calming exercises can help your rushing mind slow down and can also help you to calmly surrender and let go. Spiritual surrender is an in-depth form of powerful knowing, that, in the end, it will all be good.

"Relax. Everything is running right on schedule."
-THE UNIVERSE

It is through letting go that you can finally bid farewell to anxiety and learn to see this life in a new light, one that isn't controlled. It will be a life in which you can allow things to happen as they do, to land just where they are meant to land. It will be a life in which you can finally learn to surrender.

It's only in surrendering that we can be peaceful and free. You can sabotage success by pushing too hard. Surrender is the antidote to stress in a world that relentlessly conspires to put pressure on us, to insist on what success should be.

Letting go is the secret key to manifesting power and success in all areas of life, including work, relationships, sexuality, health, and healing. In our super-connected world, where emails, phone and text messages, and social media constantly interrupt us, it's easier to let go than you think. Learning to surrender removes the exhaustion that comes from trying too hard, and it helps you achieve goals more effortlessly, bringing ongoing happiness. I call it woodchip. If you throw a woodchip in the water, it doesn't control where it is going, it just goes with the flow and lands where it should.

WILLINGNESS

Willingness is having the integrity to let others be who they are. As humans, we want to interfere, protect, and even try to fix our loved ones. When we step back and look at the whole picture, we obtain a clearer view, which in turn gives us the ability to let each person experience his or her own life's blueprint, and with that acknowledgement, we open our eyes to our own life's blueprint. That awareness empowers our souls to just simply be. All that is required is an open mind and the willingness to do the best we can. We need that willingness to face all things, and also to know what will be will be. Having the willingness to break the cycle and be vulnerable does take courage. It also takes faith in a higher power and in oneself. We so often negate or belittle ourselves, feeling we should do more, achieve more, or strive for more, but when we stop pushing so hard, and instead we start showing ourselves compassion, we will begin to feel a truer sense of balance in our lives. We need to learn to just be. Trying to be something more just to feel better about ourselves diminishes the willingness to just be, and to love.

Now, there's a huge difference between "wanting" and "willingness" to change. Willingness is the key to change. The difference may seem subtle, but it's not. The "want to" is what is under the surface, hidden by resentment, fear, and guilt. People don't lack "want to," they lack the willingness to do what it takes to change. Sometimes, the willingness is forced on you. For years, a friend wanted to lose weight to be healthier, and to also get in shape. She knew the first step she needed to take, yet she would eat bread and butter, drink liquor, have pasta, and eat sweets. She constantly reminded me that she needed to get on a program. The "want to," she had tons of it. But it didn't matter, because she didn't have the "willingness." However, one day it was raining and she ran to her car a block away. When she entered her car and started hyperventilating, trying to catch her breath, she felt chest pains and stiffness in her left arm. She immediately drove to the emergency room, where they informed her she had had a mild heart attack. Today, she works out three times a week and she's taking care of herself. I'm not ganging up on overweight people. Lack of willingness can affect many realms—addictions to cigarettes, drugs, alcohol, gambling, shopping, etc. In fact, "wanting to" might be counterproductive, making us feel virtuous even though we're not making any real changes. The "want to" allows us to fool ourselves. "Willingness" is quite a different thing. "Willingness" means that we're ready to take action and then we do it. Willingness is intensely personal. It has to come totally from within. How do we come to have the willingness that's critical for change and improvement? For most of us, it comes when we hit some kind of low point. For some, the willingness comes about due to careful self-examination, being honest with oneself, and an ability to make difficult choices and stick to them. Either way, willingness is key.

TRUTH

The basis of truth is reality, the reality that is in front of you. The inability to see it will open the path to pain and disappointment. "The truth will set you free" is one of my favorite quotes, but knowing the truth and accepting it are two different things. It's extremely hard to lie to ourselves when we sincerely seek truth within us. When you can look in the mirror and be totally honest about whatever your issues are, the solution and recovery will have a chance to commence. You can't change the truth, but the truth can change you. Therefore, lying to oneself is fatal. With truth, we can conquer and gain strength in the here and now. I read a survey that said humans lie at least 50 times a day. I find myself to be a truthful person, but as I went back over my day, I realized I do lie. When someone asked me, "Is this a pretty blouse?" I lied and said yes. Someone else asked, "Do you like my purple hair?" I lied and said yes. It wasn't my responsibility to hurt the person's feeling with the truth of my opinion. This raises a question: honesty versus truthfulness. What I've learned is that honesty and truthfulness are two distinct terms. Honesty is only the proper choice if it is upholding truthfulness at the same time. When honesty goes against truthfulness, it takes away from the essence of who you are, and it serves as a hindrance in your personal growth.

It might seem counter-intuitive at first glance that giving up honesty could possibly be a good thing. Furthermore, it might also seem paradoxical to give up honesty in order to be truthful. Aren't these two words synonymous? While honesty is the act of not lying, truthfulness involves upholding a deeper level of truth, even if it takes some lying to achieve it. For example, the dictionary defines truth as the true or actual state of a matter, while defining honesty as being honorable in principles, intentions, and actions. People can be truthful in what they say, but not honest in their intent. I was also thinking about people who constantly lie, so much so that they believe it to be the truth. So, if they believe their lies to be the truth, does that make them honest? In conclusion, being truthful is deeper and helps with spiritual growth. The national argument right now is, 1—who's got the truth and 2—who's got the facts? Until we can manage to get the two of these back together again, we're not going to make much progress. The truth forces people to opt for deep, courageous, and generous engagement in the field of justice, as well as peace.

When I was a kid I would often lie to fit in, mainly to hide the shame of not having a great relationship with my dad. When kids would share stories of good times with their dads, like camping, fishing, or simply playing games, I would lie and say I did these things as well with my dad.

As a kid I learned the rules but not the values that would make me search for and tell the truth.

LOVE

Self-love is the core of all love. It is extremely hard to sustain love if you do not love yourself. Finding someone or something to fulfill that need for love will only accomplish a temporary ineffable happiness, which in turn leads to wanting more and more, and in time becomes resentment and disappointment. Relying on other people's opinion is like trying to look at yourself in a broken mirror.

Unconditional love without judgment, with deep and tender affection toward someone, is the ultimate reward you get when your core is fulfilled. It is easier said than done, however, and requires a lot of work. I find journaling and the mirror process, which requires a conversation with oneself in the mirror, are the best ways to start. However, don't approach the mirror with negativity, only seeing what is wrong with you physically, like my nose is too big, my hair looks awful, I have a zit. Give yourself the reinforcement that you belong here on earth; you are not here as a mistake but as a necessary component of the puzzle. You have to see all the good qualities and begin to appreciate yourself, the wonderful human being that you are.

The necessary vulnerability in a romantic relationship can lead to getting hurt, that is true. Loneliness hurts, rejection hurts, losing someone hurts, jealousy hurts. It can be a great excuse to blame these things on love. In reality, self-love is the only thing in this world that helps heal all the pain and makes us feel wonderful again. I reinforce my children with love often. I will share with you what I often say: "If I could give you one thing in life, I would give you the ability to see yourself through my eyes. Only then would you realize how special you are." Don't be afraid to love and be loved. Building a wall around your heart will in fact protect it but will also block any goodness from coming in.

ACTION

We all know that action is required to accomplish something. You want to go to the store, you have to walk, ride a bike, or get in your car—that's action. I would like to talk about something that is even more important than action, and that is reaction. What is your reaction to the action of something or someone who affects you? Someone cuts you off. Someone says something that angers you or triggers you. I believe it is controlling your reaction to things that builds your strength of self. I received a text on my phone that triggered me, and my immediate thought was, "I'm going to return the text with a swift rebuttal." Instead, I paused and thought about my reaction, asking myself why I was so triggered. This allowed me to see that my reaction was triggered by something in my past, something that needed my attention. So I never responded to that text.

Things are going to happen in life—good things, bad things, all sorts of things. How you react to them will be the key action to successfully enhancing your growth as a powerful human being. The strength it requires to pause—yes, pause, take a deep breath, exhale—can change any scenario. The books I've read on Gandhi, Martin Luther King Jr., and Nelson Mandela, to name a few, showed their extraordinary ability to control their reactions to actions taken against them. It is extremely powerful to have the inner strength not to react when you feel someone or something has hurt you or done you wrong, not to mention being arrested, beaten, and treated as they were. I urge you to work on the ability to pause and think of your reaction, because it will give you immense powers of growth. The universe gives you what you ask from your thoughts but it also gives you what you demand by your actions. Actions speak louder than words. We can apologize over and over, but if our actions don't change, the words become meaningless. At some point we have to take responsibility for our actions and reactions. Once is a fluke, twice is a coincidence, three times is a pattern. That pause, that reflection before reacting, can give us the self-awareness we need to grow and change.

> "You may never know what results
> come from your actions.
> but if you have controlled reactions,
> you can be assured that there will be better results."

TRUST

Trust is a strong reliance on yourself, another person, or a thing. Self-trust—the ability to rely on your gut feeling, intuition, or the "antenna" you were born with—can be an extremely powerful access to insight. As for trust in another person, I always say, "Trust the character of someone as opposed to the charisma." Anyone can have charisma, given the right place or setting, but it is the character of that person that should be measured, and that begins to build a foundation for trust. There is also another side to this kind of trust—having faith in something you can't see or know, putting your mind to rest by relying on the integrity and principle of the unknown. To trust the unknown, the mind has to have the ability to believe. No matter what you believe in, a power higher than your understanding or something beyond, is the key. You can trust that the universe will meet your needs, but it can only meet the needs you are willing to stand for and work toward, following each opportunity that presents itself to you. The universe works off your energy. Non-trusting, negative thoughts will attract repeated predicaments. Your spiritual journey may not always appear smooth, but when you trust that what you pray for will be given to you in the most perfect way, and that you are always guided on your journey, your trust will be abundantly rewarded.

When it comes to trust in relationships, it is important to realize that it takes time for a relationship to grow and develop. Each individual brings his or her own history in the beginning. Then the process begins, to determine if both of you are compatible enough to establish a foundation. Trust takes time to grow, and it is important to respect and give it its proper due. Keep in mind that you can lose trust and discontinue progress in any relationship. That is where your gut feelings come into play. They have been with you your whole life. Stay out of your head; it always makes sense but it can't be relied on in isolation from your gut.

*"I trust you" is a better compliment than "I love you,"
because you may not always trust the person you
love, but you can always love the person you trust.
-SPIRITUAL COMPASS*

COMPASSION

This is the emotion that one feels in response to the pain and suffering of another, which prompts a desire to help through difficult times. It's a deep awareness of their suffering and an understanding that we can be there to relieve it. What I've come to understand is that the world is never saved in grand messianic gestures, but in the simple accumulation of gentle and almost invisible acts of compassion.

It's absurd to think you can't change things but it's even more absurd to think it's foolish and unimportant to try. Another way of having compassion is for someone who has done you wrong. It's recognizing that they did not have the tools to do or know better. It doesn't mean that you approve of what they've done, but it gives you a clearer understanding. Compassion also breaks down barriers in relationships with people who challenge us. After years of working on myself I realized the difficulty I had communicating with my mom was from resentment that I hadn't gotten the attention I wanted or needed during my childhood. By trying to understand her circumstances and how difficult it must have been to get married at 15 and have kids with a man twice her age, I was able to feel compassion for her instead of resentment. This led me to try to help other people in my life.

When we see someone suffering and we are moved to help, we forget the reasons we have difficulty with the person, as our natural tendency is to let the caring take over. In these moments, we see and express only good. Compassion brings us back to ourselves. You will encounter frustrations, and losses will occur. You will make mistakes, bump up against your limitations, and you'll fall short of your ideals. This is the human condition, a reality shared by all of us.

How would your life be different, too, if you stopped making negative judgmental assumptions about people you meet and viewed them, instead, with compassion and understanding? Let today be the day you look for the good in everyone and respect their journey. Live life with compassion.

L   LET

O   OTHERS

V   VOLUNTARILY

E.   EVOLVE

**BE MINDFUL OF THE
RECEIVER OF YOUR LOVE**

SPIRITUAL COMPASS

TOLERANCE

This is having respect for, and understanding of, someone's beliefs or practices, even if they differ from yours. It is the ability to live with or put up with something or someone, even when you disagree or do things differently. I'm a believer and lover of imperfections, including my own, but

we live in a world that promotes perfection—the perfect body, the perfect house, car, spouse, children, diet, etc. However, in any relationship, what often makes it work is not expecting perfection and tolerating the other person's imperfections.

As with any spiritual learning, tolerance must be internalized before it can be expressed outwardly and put into practice with others. Tolerance of yourself is necessary if you are to be tolerant of others. If we could look into each other's hearts and understand the unique challenges each of us have faced, I think we would treat each other much more gently, with more love, patience, care, and tolerance.

It seems that nowadays there is a great amount of confusion when it comes to how to have tolerance as it relates to society, how we interact with people around us, and the leaders we choose. We are all entitled to our own choices, but we need to give respect to the dignity of others' choices. When you feel threatened, it is because you are unsure of yourself, and this makes it hard to tolerate others. We need to give others the freedom to disagree with us, including expressing their contrary viewpoints and beliefs, without their fearing punishment or retribution. Imagine a theist and an atheist who are friends, and who sometimes have friendly debates about the existence of God. They both feel strongly about their points of view but are able to tolerate these differences.

Living in a diverse and pluralistic society, we are going to encounter all sorts of different and diverse viewpoints. Rarely are we going to agree on all things. So the way to celebrate our diversity is to see the different viewpoints as actually making us stronger rather than weaker. Otherwise, think what would happen. Our intolerance leads us to arguing and fighting those who disagree with our view of reality; then, those who disagree with us are forced to fight back in self-defense. Before you know it, fighting continues between the two sides, and the society breaks out in chaos, culminating in something so horrific that the society will never be the same. For the sake of society, we have no choice but to grow in tolerance.

FORGIVENESS

To forgive means to wipe the slate clean, to pardon and to let go. It is impossible to be on this earth without getting hurt, offended, lied to, and wronged. Keep in mind that we may have hurt, offended, lied to, and wronged someone as well. We can quickly point out the wrong someone has done to us while quietly forgetting to look at our own wrongdoing.

Think of all the years you have waited for someone to "make it up to you," and all the energy you expended trying to make the person change, make him pay, or my favorite is "waiting for him to apologize." Yet the person may never change. Meanwhile, you've kept the old wounds from healing and also given pain from the past or present free rein to shape and even damage your life. Your positive, optimistic views will never have value to someone who has a negative outlook.

Inner peace is found by changing yourself and not the people who hurt you. Change yourself for yourself, for the joy, serenity, and peace of mind, understanding, compassion, laughter, and a bright future, all by forgiveness. And don't forget to forgive yourself. We beat ourselves up way too much for our past failures. This is the time to cease and forgive. It wasn't your fault, and you can't keep on carrying the burden. Forgiveness is the final act of love. Some of the greatest gifts of forgiveness are the realization of peace. You realize that no experience is ever wasted. You were never a mistake in anyone's life, and no one was ever a mistake in yours. Because no matter how long a painful experience was present in your life, it was only there the exact amount of time it needed to be.

Although having good intentions to forgive others seems to be the right thing to do, forgiveness often doesn't take away the pain or allow you to forget what certain people have said or done to you. "When you lose, don't lose the lesson". You can express to someone that you feel upset or uncomfortable with his or her behavior, saying what you mean without being mean when you say it. The more you stand up for yourself, the more open you will be to forgive and the more positive energy you can bring to your relationships. When all parties have a mutual understanding of forgiveness, then any relationship can be maintained. This spiritual awakening can also transform partnerships.

Forgiving is not forgetting; it's letting go of the hurt and the story you have been holding onto. Free yourself of the resentment.
-SPIRITUAL COMPASS

HUMILITY

Humility doesn't mean you've become a doormat or turned the other cheek. There is strength in being humble. The loudest in a room is not the strongest power. Powerful people, like Gandhi, Jesus, Martin Luther King Jr., Nelson Mandela, Mother Theresa, and the Dalai Lama, don't look strong. However, they moved the masses and changed the world. After reading many of their books, I realized that they all had humility, even in the depths of humiliation. The strength to be modest and respectful, even against fear and humiliating opposition, is so powerful. Perpetual quietness of the heart is to have no trouble, not to fret or be vexed, irritable or sore, to wonder at nothing that is done to us, to feel nothing done against us. So when nobody praises me, when I am blamed or despised, when trouble is all around me, I can go inward to the safe zone within myself where I can shut the door and be at peace. The power of humility in life is a blessing, enabling us to find meaning in life events, to pursue our individual purpose, and to be compassionate toward others.

Humility is unique to each individual, to the deepest part of you, the part that lets you make meaning of your world. It is that innermost part of you that allows you to gain strength, hope, and peace, knowing you have a purpose to fulfill.

How do we live a humble life?

Being humble does not mean counting others as more significant than ourselves, but where do our needs and desires fit in? This is a hard question. It's often easier to give in and do more than we should, because we don't want to feel someone's displeasure toward us. It's easier to feel victimized than it is to live triumphantly.

I do believe there is a way to give our needs the attention they deserve while also considering the needs of others: "pleasing people" as opposed to "people pleasing." When you please people, you put yourself first and consider your feelings to know if they fit with what you are being asked to do. Don't put yourself in a situation where you people please and then you are nowhere to be found. This builds disappointment and resentment, leaving you asking yourself why you said "yes" when you really wanted to say "no."

Just like on an airplane, we have to remember to put the mask on ourselves first before we put one on someone else. When you choose to be motivated by self-focus and self-love, you keep your heart open to honesty and humility.

PERSPECTIVE

Perspective is your way of thinking and seeing things from your point of view. Imagine we are both looking at a building, but you are in a helicopter looking down at it while I am at ground level looking up. To you, the building looks small and for me, the building looks big. Our views are different. For instance, you have a better perspective for gaining information about the roof of the building while I have a better perspective for counting the number of wood panels on the door. We may have different perspectives, but the fact still remains that we are both looking at the same building. When we can recognize that our perspective and someone else's both have value, we can then become open to respecting the other person's point of view.

We are so sensitive to our own emotions yet so insensitive and intolerant of others' feelings. This is when it is time to break free and see things from a larger perspective, one other than our own. When something bad happens, you have three choices. You can either let it define you, let it destroy you, or you can let it strengthen you. It's all about your perspective, of seeing the bigger picture. Try to keep in mind that people may not understand your perspective and feelings unless you've clearly explained them. Things that are clear from where you stand may be completely invisible from someone else's perspective. If you do explain and they still don't get it or just don't care, then it doesn't mean you've wasted your time; it simply means you now know for sure that you won't be thoroughly valued, understood, or considered, if at all, by this person.

"We can complain that rose bushes have thorns or we can rejoice that rose bushes have roses."
—ABRAHAM LINCOLN

Sometimes, a change of perspective is all we need to see the world as it really is, and to take responsibility for our own actions. We begin to learn how to nurture our mental and spiritual growth from a new vantage point. Success and failure are a matter of perspective. Even in difficult situations, realizing that we do achieve many small successes every day allows us to challenge old ideas that limit us and gives us opportunities to learn wonderful things about ourselves.

EVERYONE WANTS THREE
THINGS:
TO BE HEARD
TO BE SEEN
TO BE LOVED
WHEN WE DO NOT GET ONE OR
ALL THREE WE GET TRIGGERED,
BUT IT MUST BEGIN WITH YOU.
LOOK IN THE MIRROR AND LET
THIS BE YOUR MANTRA
I HEAR YOU
I SEE YOU
I LOVE YOU

SPIRITUAL COMPASS

INSIGHT

Having insight is the ability to gain a deep and intuitive understanding of a person, phenomenon, or yourself. Our experiences in life enlighten our insight into familiar situations. As life goes on, we develop our spiritual insight, which is also referred to as our sixth sense, the intuitive side that we all have. It's an advantage we humans have over technology. Computers don't have gut feelings about things but we do, and can make well-chosen decisions based on our intuition. My grandmother used to call this penetrating, sudden understanding of a situation or problem «the blind eye." Some people are given the insight of a psychic. One of my friends had this ever since childhood. His mom was startled when he told her to "call grandma. She's not feeling well." Suddenly the phone rang. It was a nurse from the hospital. Grandma had fallen and broken her wrist. We all have some measure of this insight. In any moment of decision, pay attention to your insight and gut feeling; they've been with you since your birth and may provide the truest understanding of your choices.

Meditation and journaling can help you gain insight. During meditation you enter into deep thought, where you can develop specific questions you'd like answers to, or gain insights into what these might mean for you and your life path. The insights we receive in meditation can often be subtle and vague until we explore them more completely. This is where journaling can help us develop clarity about our life and spiritual path, giving us a better understanding of the subtle nudges from our inner wisdom. This deeper understanding, with both your mind and heart, helps you trust the universe that everything is happening just as it should.

COMMITMENT

In today's society, commitment is uncommon. We live in a culture where there's always something brighter and newer around the corner, and where the fruits of commitment are rarely seen. Most people find it less and less appealing. They perceive things that don't require commitment to be more fulfilling than they actually might be, and are confused about what to commit to. In relationships, fear without the availability of comfort and commitment can lead to separation and isolation, creating stress. Healthy relationships of any kind are activated when we have "self-commitment, the determination to develop ourselves" recognizing that being part of someone's life is more realistic than being their entire life. Self-commitment requires the determination to make whatever change we feel we need, whether our goal is to have dedication, be more friendly and outgoing, to lose weight, or anything else. We all know subconsciously that the struggle with commitment diminishes when we can let go of things that don't serve us any longer, such as being a doormat in an abusive or non-meaningful relationship. Before committing and jumping into any situation or relationship, you need strong boundaries and controlled expectations.

Committing because it sounds good or you think it will work itself out is just silly. This applies to all commitments of our mind, body, and soul. Every New Year I see people start going to the gym with full dedication, and yet after two to three months they quit. Many people say, "I'll work on myself, my mental and spiritual growth," without realizing it requires preparation and sacrifice to fully commit and maintain that commitment. My slogan is, "If it doesn't fit, don't commit." It's a big deal to take on a commitment without due consideration. There is a difference between interest and commitment. When you are interested in doing something, you do it when it's convenient. When you are committed to something, you accept no excuses, only full participation. Without commitment, you cannot have depth in anything, whether in a relationship, a business, or a hobby. Commitment is at the very heart of what it means to be fully engaged.

It is the daily triumph of integrity that transforms the promise into reality. Committing boldly to your own happiness requires a habit of discipline, which is to not abandon the practice of self-love. Of course, you can't expect to be happy all the time, but at every obstacle, you can try to change your attitude. To make the decision that happiness is an inside job and much of the time we can choose to be happy.

> If you think the sky is the limit, let me remind you there are human footprints on the moon. NEVER QUIT. Go further and bigger.
> –SPIRITUAL COMPASS

JOY

We all speak of joy and wish for joy in our lives, yet we don't fully understand the true meaning of joy in the context of spirituality and the work of our soul, confusing joy with happiness. Spiritual joy is a state of the heart and the soul. It is produced when the heart and soul unite in the service of a greater good. It creates within a person a sense of contentment, acceptance, and serenity, a deep knowledge that whatever might happen, it will all be for the highest and greatest good. Happiness is different. Happiness is a state of delight and emotional well-being in which you feel completely without stress and anxiety. You focus only on the good, the positive, celebrating each moment of your life. Happiness is the ideal that we are all striving for, that we find in a favorite book, house, car, friend, partner, flowers—whatever makes you happy. Joy produces spiritual fortitude and strength. Joy is outward-focused. We want to bring joy to the world, as the song says. Volunteering to build a dam for fresh water; reading to kids in a reading program; giving out water or running in a cancer run/walk; simply making someone smile—these give us that fulfillment which brings a certain unexplainable joy to our heart. I recently volunteered to give free packed lunches to the homeless. The way the hungry little girls smiled with happiness for an apple brought the biggest joy to my heart. Joyfulness in the heart is so powerful. We need to give each other the room to grow, to be ourselves, and to exercise our diversity in pursuit of what gives us joy and brings joy to others. When we do this, we all receive beautiful gifts—ideas, openness, dignity, healing, inclusion, and most of all joy. We can have a boundless amount of joy in just being alive. We can't cling endlessly to happiness, trying to freeze time to hold onto it. If our joy is snatched away, it is not forever. By letting go of that fear, we become freer to experience and fully enjoy those precious moments of joy.

COLORS

Colors are so powerful. Spiritual colors go even deeper. For example, yellow is usually irritating, however, spiritually, it's inspiring and joyful. Red means excitement and hunger; for example, most fast-food restaurants have red in their logos. However, its spiritual meaning is humility. That being said, the colors of the Spiritual Compass express these deeper meanings of the colors. As humans, we have unique emotional responses to colors. For example, why does one person love green and another finds it disgusting? When you engage deeper into understanding who you are spiritually, you will begin to have a different perspective on how you feel about yourself and how things affect you, such as colors and your surroundings. We manifest our being as we peel the onion, so to speak, and we discover who we truly are. Then, the people and things around us feel different, even though everyone and everything remains the same, because internally we are the ones who have changed.

There are two ways we access knowledge: through concepts and experience. For example, parents, teachers, mentors, family, or friends may tell us that green is the color of the forest or beautiful plants and trees, but when we go out into the wilderness, we experience the forest. We feel the sensation of being in the midst of the experience. I hope that as you explore and engage in the Spiritual Compass, you take the time to feel every color as it affects you daily. I have researched the colors of the Spiritual Compass to bring you a stronger awareness of their true essence and emotional depth. I experienced this encounter with color when I was in Greece, where the color of the water is so captivating—a rich, deep blue-green with a hint of aqua—absolutely stunning. I gazed at it as if it had been a painting, letting it affect all my senses. I strongly recommend taking a trip there!

SPIRITUALITY

Spirituality is not a sudden burst of insight or powerful experience, like the Biblical episode of the burning bush. Instead, it's a gradual journey to knowing that you are not alone in the universe. That belief in a higher existence is an energy-driven force that can give you the awareness to make your life joyous and productive. A spiritual awakening can happen at any time along your journey toward a "came to believe" moment. It confirms for you that your being on this planet is not by mistake or that you're just passing through, but rather you are a blessing to this planet, accomplishing things, giving, receiving, and most importantly, growing. I created the Spiritual Compass as a guide to bring you back to your power, the power within you, your eternal bright light that needs only to be turned on. It has always been there, but you may have let it dim or let others blow it out. I encourage you to make this your time to begin your journey of illumination. Now, how do you do this at a time when you may feel overwhelmed, hurting, or uneasy? Be still and take a breath. Ask your higher power for help to see the bigger picture that is planned for you, meditating on the insight to appreciate the beautiful things around you—a bright-eyed baby, a majestic tree, flowers, a puppy, the sound of birds. And pray.

The Serenity Prayer

God, grant me the serenity
to accept the things that I cannot change,
the courage to change the things that I can,
and the wisdom to know the difference.

I use this prayer as a reminder, but you may prefer to make up your own prayer or to use a prayer you are familiar with or that you've encountered somewhere. The most important thing is having that connection. It is about having options to enhance your spiritual experience

Fear can be a spiritual stumbling block and cause us to feel stuck. That is when I urge you to stop and ask yourself what you are fearful about. Ask to know the core of it. When we do that, we can go back and see where it started and then we can start planning a solution. Spirituality gives us the willingness to believe that our Higher power will take care of us. That's how strong spirituality is, a harmonious energy that makes us equal partners in a spiritual enterprise. Respecting each other's participation allows us to practice the golden rule of treating others the way we would like to be treated. We are all part of an orchestra with a conductor, and we can all play different instruments and sets of notes, but it all blends to make beautiful music.

Be Aware of your thoughts and feelings. They impact your moods and external realities.
-SPIRITUAL COMPASS

RELATIONSHIP

There are many kinds of relationships, but in our society we concentrate more on romantic relationships. They are considered the most meaningful source of deep fulfillment. This need for human connection appears as early as the story of Adam. Although he had an amazing garden, he asked for a partner, to have a relationship. From early childhood, we have learned to rely on whoever is our caregiver. That relationship gives us our experiences of being taken care of, protected, ignored, or abused, creating patterns of relating with others.

Every relationship requires an investment of time, emotion, and energy, whether relating with a Higher power, as a couple, with parents, children, siblings, employers, co-workers, or friends. Having the integrity to be you, no matter what, is the key to keeping your individuality and importance in any relationship. Self-respect allows you to ask for what you need and encourage others to do the same. Expecting people to read your mind, or putting pressure on them to validate you, is a tall order. The need to dominate and control others will lead to a difficult or failed relationship.

Most of us have to work consciously to acquire the skills necessary to make relationships endure and flourish. The process of building a strong foundation takes time, because we all have our own ideas, values, and upbringing that won't always mesh with those of the other person. Kindness and respect for everyone involved will deepen any relationship. I have created a list of things I want and that are important to me in a relationship:

1. Chemistry
2. Communication
3. Compatibility
4. Consideration
5. Consistency

I call these my "Five Cs," but you can create your own. The key is to know what you want or need. There is something to learn from every interaction with someone else. Having acceptance while still taking care of your own needs, however, is a great practice.

The last part of relationship is the one you have with yourself. When you want to criticize yourself and have thoughts of not being enough and not deserving to be loved, I would suggest you pause and take a deep breath. You are unique and special. No one is like you. Believe in yourself. Go to the mirror and repeat after me:

"I see you"
"I hear you"
"I love you"

The strongest relationship should be with yourself, so nurture and care for the most amazing human being, which is YOU. As we live our lives, we have the opportunity to work on ourselves to have growth, emotionally, mentally, and spiritually.

PEOPLE PLEASING

People pleasing is disgusting and repulsive, because it means you put other people first. You become a carpet where you allow others to walk all over you, slamming the door on you whenever they feel like it. We know deep down that those behaviors are uncalled for, but we want to be liked. I used to want to help others and be the hero at any cost. I wanted people to like me for what I did rather than who I was. I was walking around with a barrel of giving and when you do that, you attract users. Your feelings are either dismissed or ignored, and you become resentful because you are not appreciated or getting the validation you seek. Constantly "doing" rather than "being" never allows your true attributes to shine. I was looking outside myself for approval and my manipulative ways made it an obsession. It kept me distracted from focusing on my self-worth, self-esteem, and self-respect. I also would judge my value by accomplishments—the best job, car, house, jewelry, clothing, or smartest points of view. I had to be the center of attention, and all that energy exhausted and depressed me. I couldn't just be myself.

We all have an instinctive need to fit in, expecting our approval to come from other people, which never fills the void we feel. I told myself that I was no longer going to be a doormat. I took some time to reflect on my behavior, and it came to a point where I realized that "people pleasing" is a bad thing, but "pleasing people" is, in fact, healthy. It meant that I would put myself first and pause before I did something for someone else. Doing things without looking for appreciation lets you know you're doing it for the right reasons. As you practice this technique, you become more aware of your behavior and begin to fine-tune your responses. You no longer say "yes" when you really want to say "no." The beauty of building self-worth this way is that it opens your perspective to let others have the privilege to choose themselves first as well.

There is much to learn about ourselves by noticing the individuals we choose to surround us. Choosing friends who are kind and positive helps to create healthy boundaries. It slowly dissolves the patterns from early childhood created by lack of nurture, emotional instability, and lack of safety. These patterns are often ingrained and can be extremely difficult to break. Nonetheless, we must learn coping skills that will help us avoid and break them. These skills are what I learned in therapy and recovery. You can sand the toolbox, spray paint it, put new tools in it, but remember, YOU are still in charge of the toolbox. YOU have to continuously find the tools that work for you, such as journaling, meditation, therapy, and practicing self-love.

People pleasing is awful. It builds resentment. You did not put yourself first. You said yes when you wanted to say no. Pleasing people is when you put yourself first You said no when it was necessary.
    -SPIRITUAL COMPASS

PERSONAL RESPONSIBILITY

We are all born with the ability to know the difference between right and wrong. However, we are also born with free will, which means that even though we know a behavior is wrong, we might do it anyway. Recognizing our personal responsibility in every situation allows us to live in the reality in front of us. Blind reliance upon "experts" and uncritical acceptance of popular catchwords and prejudices amount to neglecting self-determination and giving in to other people's rules and control. This practice can cause us to evade personal responsibility and feel blameless. We neglect to examine our role in situations and outcomes. Here is an example. After dropping my friend at the airport in her car, I returned to her place to move my car, which was parked at a limited-time space. I parked her car on the side of the road and left it running while I got in my car and waited for a parking space to open up. It dawned on me to turn off her car, but I convinced myself that a space would open soon. After a while I noticed a man enter her car and take off. I immediately started chasing him and after a few U-turns at high speed I decided to ram my car into her car. As we both spun, he hit a bus, got out of the car, and ran. I got out of my car and immediately fell to the ground. I had torn my patellar tendon. Police were called and ten officers appeared. It was chaos. While in the emergency room, I realized my personal responsibility. I should have parked her car legally, removed the keys, and waited for a proper parking space for my car. In this situation it would have been easy to feel I was a victim, living in blame, justification, and rationalization. Instead, I had the awareness to recognize my part in the chaos. Many of us see ourselves as innocent victims. It can be shocking to us when we see our share in hurting others and ourselves, but with that recognition, we develop a more accurate sense of reality.

Personal responsibility is also taking care of self in a loving, kind way. After all, you are the main event of your life. I call it "respond-ability." How are you responding to you and your needs? Are you setting proper boundaries? Are you letting resentment take over? Are you giving up your power to someone else? Are you stopping to smell the roses? This awareness of personal respond-ability will enhance your freedom and personal power. It's your responsibility to take care of your own feelings.

It is the wounded self that goes to the defensive position of faulting others, rather than to the positive of responsibility. Fault can imply wrong or bad, whereas responsibility implies accountability for your choices and the consequences. When we resist taking personal responsibility, in all areas of our lives, we limit the frequency and abundance of awareness that help us access a higher source of guidance that can expand our freedom, personal power, and joy. It's not always easy, but it's always worth it. This works in all areas of your life, including your responsibility to take time for playing and having fun, because they will bring balance into your life.

Taking responsibility for yourself makes you realize that you are not responsible for the entire universe. I have a note on my refrigerator that says:

"Hi, this is GOD.
I will be handling all things today.
I will not need your help, so have a good day."

It is a reminder to release myself from responsibility when appropriate, and to trust my higher power. I am powerless over many things, and should keep the focus on what I can control: myself, and whatever is my personal responsibility.

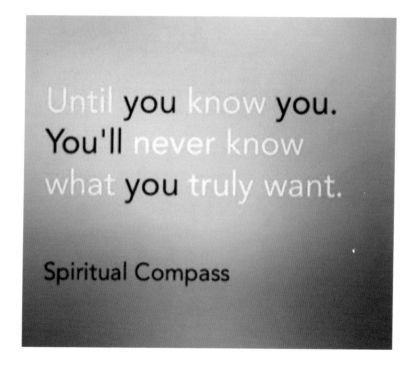

Until you know you. You'll never know what you truly want.

Spiritual Compass

SELF-CRITICISM

As humans, we are frequently critical of ourselves. Our inner critic is a collection of negative voices from our past, and when we listen to these voices, they become damaging to our opinions of ourselves. We use the mirror to criticize our hair, face, bodies, and our inner mirror to judge our capabilities. We tell ourselves that we are not good enough; comparison and despair allow doubt and shame to creep in. Emotional self-abuse can be devastating. As a child, you collect and absorb attitudes that influence your inner dialogue. Parents, kids at school, teachers, counselors, coaches, adults who disempowered you, and all types of physical, sexual, verbal, and emotional abuse, often create the pain within us.

It's not unusual to wear a metaphorical »armor" that hides ourselves, to feel safe when we are at work, at social gatherings, or in unfamiliar situations. It's called "putting on our best face." When you see kids, you know exactly what their emotions are by their body language; there is no hiding. As adults, we think we have mastered the art of controlling our body language, but that's the chink in the armor. We have a lot of body language that we just can't hide: clenched teeth, big sighs, angry eyebrows, crossed arms, etc. It's mostly a reactive behavior. Isn't it high time we made amends with ourselves, started believing in ourselves, and removed the stranglehold of past hurts and disappointments? You have to get rid of that mind chatter. It can begin with finding one thing that you like about yourself in the mirror. Then, find another. There is no time frame. I'm not asking you to make an entire list today, but gradually to build on the good things: your eyes, lips, brows, teeth, hands, height, nose, etc. When you identify those positive qualities, you can accept compliments with gentleness and compassion for yourself. I told an older woman how pretty her sundress was, and she replied, "Oh please, it's not new." I told her, "Old or new, you look great," and she finally smiled and accepted the compliment. You can make this wise choice to develop a safe and trusting relationship with yourself, dropping the mask of gloom and doom, rejoicing in the beautiful, unique, and powerful being you already are. It's about being brave enough to take a chance and believe in yourself.

"Perfection is the killer of good."

Getting out of the need for perfection will get you into the awareness that self-doubt and self-criticism are just perceptions that can be changed. Self-compassion beats self-criticism every day.

There is a further benefit from self-compassion: It supports self-improvement, which can help you make further changes. Something we can all do when we need a little encouragement and motivation is to write for three minutes, from a compassionate and understanding perspective, because there is a power when pen hits paper. Doing this will help remove negative feelings and also get you out of blaming yourself for your anxiety and self-criticism.

CONTROL

Everywhere you turn, there is some control issue, whether it is self-control, mind control, birth control, remote control, out of control, climate control, cruise control, etc. We get caught up in the delusion that we are in control. On any given day, at a supermarket or store, you may feel in control but you can't control the cashier's forgetting an item, the bag's ripping and your groceries falling all over the place, losing your keys, or getting in an accident. So the reality is that we are not in control. My friend worked hard to raise her daughter the right way, nurtured her in a private school, gave attention, controlled her whereabouts, her cell phone, and computers, and told her about the birds and the bees. Her daughter was great, but what her mother couldn't control was her daughter's meeting a friend in school, trying meth, becoming addicted, spending years going in and out of rehab, and then dying from an overdose. We can try to manipulate and control, but the outcome will be what it will be.

I will be the first to tell you that I am a controller. I tried to control people, places, and things. I realized I really didn't have any control like a weather person trying to control the temperature, saying, "Sunny days ahead," and then it would rain. The core of the reason is that I was trying to feel safe. If I controlled everything, I believed I was safe. This impossible feat was exhausting and never worked. What I can do is show up, be the best version of me, and live in the reality in front of me; be vulnerable, trust the universe and that my higher power has my back, and whatever is supposed to be will be. This doesn't mean I don't work hard or have goals and things I want, but knowing I don't control the outcome relieved me of being disappointed. Back in the 1960s, Dr. William Glasser found that people try to control when they are not getting their basic needs met. These are the 5 needs:

1) Power, or a sense of self-worth and achievement.

2) Love and belonging, or being part of a family or community of loved ones.

3) Freedom or independence.

4) Fun, which includes a sense of satisfaction or pleasure.

5) Survival or the comfort of knowing that one's basic needs of food, shelter, and sex are met.

Lacking one or more of these results in trying to control current situations or relationships. You cannot change or control others, so, the only sensible thing is to control yourself and your own behavior.

THE POWER OF SURRENDER
If you feel in a rut today, it will only vanish once you realize that resistance can only be conquered by letting go.

FEAR

Fear—where does it come from and why does it sometimes dominate your life? How do some people navigate through the fear and come out the other side even happier? Yes, it's possible that the best things in life are on the other side of fear.

A healthy acronym is **f.e.a.r.: f**alse **e**vidence **a**ppearing **r**eal. Clearly, fear can dominate our thoughts, but learning not to let it control you is important. All emotions are valid, including fear. They all have a seat in the car, they are just not allowed to drive. Don't allow that pesky feeling of fear to arise when you are at your most vulnerable.

The part of your brain known as the brain stem sends a distress signal, prompting the release of stress hormones, causing physiological changes such as increased heartbeat, sweating, breath quickening, and muscle tensing. This results in the classic responses of fight, flight, or freeze. It roots itself deep within you, telling stories that seem so real that your body responds almost automatically with a change in behavior. Fear can lead us to procrastinate, hide, and avoid confrontation, or run away from threats.

When I was younger, I saw my mom's fear of being in an elevator, and my fear of scary movies like "Pet Cemetery" or "The Exorcist." When I became older, it was the fear of playing sports, not fitting in with the kids in school, and peer pressure. Even later, it became worry, self-doubt, poor self-esteem, and fear of failure. Perhaps it's not fear itself that you need to address, but how you carry the fear.

Fear will always be a part of life, but it doesn't have to consume your life. If fear is simply removed, how are we to know the courage we have inside? A lot of worry is focused on future events, things that might happen, but if we learn to stay in the present and live one day at a time, we can ward off the effects of fear.

I decided to begin living fearlessly by believing in a higher power. No matter what fear I encountered, I decided I would trust that if I stayed where my feet were and dealt with what was in front of me without future-tripping, I would be okay. I acknowledged my fear, and I began to keep a journal. It slowly evolved in a way that gave me strength and encouragement, and it also helped me to see the big picture. It enabled me to track my progress as I worked toward conquering my fear.

After accepting and admitting my fear, I made it a point to meditate every day when I woke up, thinking about the sound of ocean waves against the rocks as I breathed in healing air and breathed out unnecessary thoughts of fearful feelings. I became astounded by the increasing calmness and stillness in my mind.

We are guided by our emotions, mainly our gut instinct, and it can serve us well if we listen to it.

Once you are clear on the source of your fear, take action. It can be the hardest, but also the most important step. Sometimes that means taking action in the direction you fear the most, knowing that, deep down, it is what you need to do.

There are challenges in life but using fear as your tour guide rather than your adversary will help you tackle those challenges. You can't defeat fear being scared of fear. Taking positive steps will guide you to a life of fulfillment, happiness, and joy.

"Fear is an unreliable power that only works
in its proximity. The further away you
get from it, the less it controls you."
-SPIRITUAL COMPASS

It is challenging to act when your gripped by
fear, start small. Each step you take into fear will
strengthen you and help you confront fears with
poise, courage, and confidence. When you stare your
fear in the face you realize that you are powerful.
-SPIRITUAL COMPASS

ENVIRONMENT

What are your surroundings? The conditions that you live or work in influence how you feel, your mood and well-being. Sometimes we go about our day and we feel off, not settled, and we can't figure out why. I challenge you to take a look at your environment. Who is constantly around you at home, work, or just hanging out? Friends you get together with—are you brainstorming or blame-storming. Negativity is a silent assassin to the soul. It creeps in as advice, opinions, good intensions, and it loves company. We ignore it for many reasons: We have known someone for a long time; we are people pleasing by not wanting to say anything, afraid to be alone—whatever the case is. Is your house filled with negative energy, pictures, art, color of paint, etc.? Do you have unhealthy food, snacks, or paraphernalia? When we don't pay attention to our environment, we may not see the lack of positive influences that we should have around us. Have things around you that inspire growth in this journey of life. Slowly remove those influences of negative people and things. A hostile environment is hard on communication, harmony, proper behavior, and the comfort just to relax. It alters the conditions. The mood or tone of your surroundings is in your control, so decide to have serenity. After all, it is your life; you're the main event. A spiritual environment brings in your belief in a higher power to help you understand and recognize how to obtain this unique environment. Once you appreciate this spiritual environment, it is possible to interact with like-minded people with a greater essence of openness.

SOCIAL MEDIA

In 1835, Justus von Liebig, using a thin layer of metallic silver behind a glass pane, invented the mirror. Even before that, we saw our reflection in still water, and back in 2000 B.C., polished bronze and copper were used as mirrors. Humans have always had an interest in their reflection.

Fast forward to today when we can take pictures and videos of ourselves right on our devices. Social media can amplify who you are—whether you are insecure, an addictive personality, fear based, a follower of conspiracy theories, controlling, positive, inspirational, or just a good person. However, social media can also be deceptive as to your identity. It's easy to hide, showing only the best picture out of all the pictures you took to portray the "best life," even if your life is in disarray, to seek validation or as it's called, "likes." It's easy to lie or be fake, because there is no accountability. The constant seeking of these "likes" can disappoint and exhaust people, causing extreme fluctuations in levels of adrenalin, endorphins, serotonin, and dopamine, affecting the body both physically and mentally.

Social media can let you take the easy and even lazy way out of real social interaction by just sending a text. When you continuously use social media or just texting, there is no true connection socially. When we talk, or have a physical interaction, a powerful part of the brain is activated. It is easy to be hypocritical and look at all the negatives of social media; I do send my mom and kids a heart and smiley emoji once in a while. Like everything else in life, moderation is the key. That's why our devices have a screen-time monitor.

EXCUSES
EXCUSES EXCUSES

The most typical excuses are loaded with explanation, justification, and rationalization. Excuses are one size fits all. They build on each other and create their own reality. This concept of an excuse is often connected to those who are hurt, angry, or frustrated, or to gain sympathy or minimize culpability. Excuses keep us from fulfilling our potential and do not excuse our personal behavior and responsibility. No problem can be solved unless a person acknowledges and admits what he has done. I once got a ticket for running a red light. Luckily the traffic photo didn't show my face, because I was reaching back for my phone that had fallen. Nonetheless, I had to deal with the ticket in court. The judge let everyone know that if the picture is unclear or it's not you, simply say it's not you and it will be dismissed, but if your face can clearly be seen, you will be charged the fine. It was so amusing to hear people's creative excuses; no one wanted to admit it was his or her fault. But I *had* to take responsibility for my actions, and am grateful to this day that no one was hurt by my actions.

So how do we work on or cure ourselves of making excuses? We can start by not blaming insufficiencies in our lives on parents, partners, bad bosses, co-workers, racism, sexism, a bad event in our past, society, or bad luck. Using these as excuses and professing it's never our fault diminishes our capacity for self-improvement and growth. It's easy for me to tell you to stop blaming and making excuses. I understand that after repeated failure, to continuously blame one-self. However, perhaps we can focus on how we can succeed despite the failures. Think of this: The most successful people don't usually blame others for their failures. We can work on preventing negative thoughts and feelings from driving our need for excuses.

GRATITUDE

Your life is a miracle. Perhaps you can't see it because you have fear, worry, doubt, or you feel alone, but when you take a moment to reflect on what you can be grateful for, and you concentrate on what you do have as opposed to what you don't have, the attitude is in the gratitude. If you can gradually learn to appreciate the small accomplishments of your daily life, it will deepen your sense of gratitude. All the gifts, talents, and wonderful things that can happen at any time to anyone will remind you to appreciate and not succumb to self-pity. Believing in your strengths will give you the opportunity to diminish the things you consider your weaknesses. Even in the darkest experiences and situations, you can find a bright light of gratitude.

Psychologists have found that feelings of gratitude increase happiness, and also build both physical and psychological health, even among those already struggling with mental health problems. Studies show that practicing gratitude curbs the use of words expressing negative emotions, and it shifts inner attention away from negative emotions such as resentment and envy, minimizing the possibility of ruminating over them.

The beneficial effects snowball over time. Brain scans of people assigned a task that stimulates expression of gratitude show lasting changes in the prefrontal cortex, which heighten sensitivity to future experiences of gratitude.

We live in a materialistic culture that promotes constant wanting and sees possessions as the source of happiness, which only creates more cynicism and narcissistic patterns, which in time diminish a place to have gratitude. Gratitude can build great expressive and emotional strength in all your relationships. Negative thinking, on the other hand, can be very destructive to your life, causing you to feel tired, sick, stressed, or unhappy with yourself or others. You can silence those thoughts of discontent by meditating on things you could appreciate and be thankful for.

"Adversity doesn't build character, it reveals it."

The key is to refuse self-pity, choosing instead to appreciate the beauty in your everyday life by reflecting gratitude for the small things and then increasing to bigger things. That is the foundation of a life of harmony.

Instead of focusing on what you don't have, I challenge you to focus on what you are grateful for today.
–SPIRITUAL COMPASS

FUN

We would all agree that fun lifts stress from us. It refreshes us and recharges us. It re-establishes our hopefulness and changes our perspective. It renews our ability to accomplish the responsibilities of the world. Society tells us to be hardworking and goal-oriented. We become so consumed with being adults, but there is no rule that says you have to stop having child-like fun. In fact, if you are able to feed the inner child, it stimulates creativity and renews the neural connections to your brain. I'm not talking about going to Vegas and having adult fun, although that may feed other needs.

Whether you had a fun childhood or no fun at all because of responsibilities of being an adult early, learning to feed the inner child is beneficial. It doesn't have to cost money. You can play hide-and-go-seek, have a tug of war or pillow fight, toss a football, fly a kite, blow bubbles, or play catch with a baseball.

It was warm and rainy when I visited my mom in Florida. I went outside, closed my eyes, and let the rain hit my face. I even stuck my tongue out. The rest of the day, I felt light and happy that I had fed my inner child.

You don't have to justify your existence by being serious and useful all the time. Try to have a fun play time once a month and see if you can increase it a little at a time, eventually it becomes part of a weekly fun time. Don't listen to that inner voice that says, I'm too old. I'll just stay home and watch television or read a book." You are never too old. I went to a kid's party and the grandparents were the clowns. They were having so much fun that they got us all throwing water balloons. In essence, they motivated us to let go and have fun. One of the things that prevents us from having fun is feeling we haven't reached our goal of success; we believe we don't deserve to have fun. Well, I am here to tell you to get over yourself. Stop beating yourself with a bat and use a feather instead. Having fun will reignite your self-worth and self-belief. I'm talking about fun at length because of its effect in all parts of our lives, including romantic relationships or marriages. Everyone does the obligatory part in the relationship and sometimes that can be routinely comfortable. Sure, schedules, work commute, perhaps kids and their schedules can take up time. You plan vacations for fun and spending time, but I'm talking about simple things like tickling or running through the sprinklers, even playing a simple card game before bed. You can easily say it is silly, but that kid-like fun can spark some unexpected fun. Relating and socializing as a couple can also be fun. Some people find being with others fun. Even if you are introverted and find it challenging, just try. It will be a great way you can both enjoy friendship together. Volunteering together is another source of "fun," improving the world in some way together. As I mentioned, I serve the homeless once a week at the Midnight Mission, and every time, I bring someone with me. We have fun talking and serving. Going to the pet shelter, playing with the pets, even if you don't adopt, sparks fun. The possibilities are endless.

SPIRITUAL
COMPASS

WORKBOOK

"The Beginning is always at this very moment."
—Spiritual Compass

HOW TO USE THE SPIRITUAL COMPASS

(I highly recommend obtaining a journal.)

1. Be in a quiet place.
   (If in your car, please pull over.)
2. Inhale a deep breath and hold, then release and repeat three times.
3. Look at the compass and let your eyes and heart lead you energetically to a point on the compass (higher power, surrender, love, trust, etc.). Then read the passage. This can be done as much as needed. Our feelings and emotions may shift during the day.
4. Take a self-inventory-write in your journal or in the space provided below:

A. Mental (current mindset)

B. Emotional (current feelings)

C. Physical (are you tired, energetic, relaxed, etc.?)

5. **RELATIONSHIP** (with self and others)

Self-write a brief description of how you perceive yourself. Describe your relationship with others (family, co-workers, significant other, spouse, etc.)

6. **FULCRUM CHARACTER TRAITS**—There are three characters: Who we think we are, who we want others to believe we are, and who we really are. These are usually forged from the early years of our childhood into who we are in the present. Whether they are set firmly or not depends on our thinking. Using this fulcrum method will show you where your strength and weakness lie. The goal is to create an awareness of what to work on.

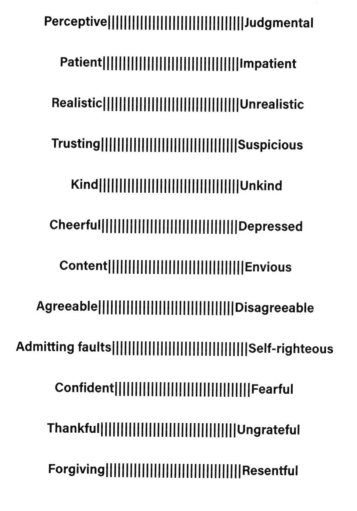

Perceptive||||||||||||||||||||||||||||||||||Judgmental

Patient|||||||||||||||||||||||||||||||||||Impatient

Realistic|||||||||||||||||||||||||||||||||||Unrealistic

Trusting|||||||||||||||||||||||||||||||||||Suspicious

Kind|||||||||||||||||||||||||||||||||||Unkind

Cheerful|||||||||||||||||||||||||||||||||||Depressed

Content|||||||||||||||||||||||||||||||||||Envious

Agreeable|||||||||||||||||||||||||||||||||||Disagreeable

Admitting faults|||||||||||||||||||||||||||||||||||Self-righteous

Confident|||||||||||||||||||||||||||||||||||Fearful

Thankful|||||||||||||||||||||||||||||||||||Ungrateful

Forgiving|||||||||||||||||||||||||||||||||||Resentful

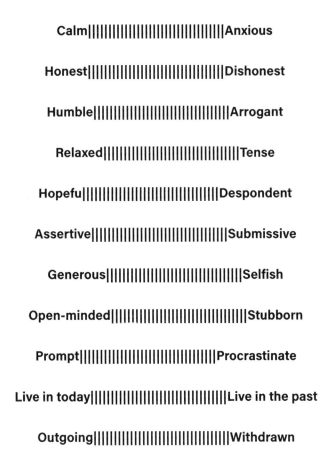

Calm||||||||||||||||||||||||||||||||Anxious

Honest||||||||||||||||||||||||||||||||||Dishonest

Humble||||||||||||||||||||||||||||||||||||Arrogant

Relaxed||||||||||||||||||||||||||||||||||||Tense

Hopefu||||||||||||||||||||||||||||||||||||Despondent

Assertive|||||||||||||||||||||||||||||||||Submissive

Generous|||||||||||||||||||||||||||||||||Selfish

Open-minded||||||||||||||||||||||||||||||||||Stubborn

Prompt|||||||||||||||||||||||||||||||||Procrastinate

Live in today|||||||||||||||||||||||||||||||||||Live in the past

Outgoing|||||||||||||||||||||||||||||||||Withdrawn

Once you recognize where you are, you can begin to improve your relationship with yourself and others. It's progress and not perfection. Write a summary of your findings.

7. SUMMARY OF FINDINGS

My positive character traits:

My negative character traits:

8. **MAKE A SELF-CARE LIST** (sleep, eat, exercise, play, have fun, laugh, etc.)

    A.

    B.

    C.

    D.

    E.

F.

G.

H.

I.

J.

9. **MAKE A GRATITUDE LIST**—There is always something to be grateful for. Just because I'm encouraging you to write a gratitude list doesn't make it a chore; it should be something you want to do. Gratitude is an integral part of your serenity. It's not the high you feel when your instant gratification is fulfilled. It is a reminder of what you have rather than what you don't have.

How to make a gratitude list.

A. Find a quiet place.

B. Be in the moment, reflecting on things that matter to you.

C. Don't focus on the past or the future, which can bring feelings of disappointment, anxiety, even fear.

D. Select a place to keep your gratitude list.

E. It's better to write it down, since a mental gratitude list is not as concrete as written.

F. Keep the format easy and make it fun.

G. Think of anything you are grateful for.

H. Add inspirational quotes, stories or pictures that bring more vibrant feelings and thoughts.

I. Include acceptance—the willingness to care for yourself.

J. Convince yourself that it is right here and right now, and you are okay.

K. The more you focus on the gratitude, the more the possibility to be more positive, which can change your perspective.

L. Keep your gratitude list updated.

Gratitude List:

10. **DAILY ROUTINE**—Consistency is the base for success. When you routinely start your day inspirationally, you can have a foundation to proceed with your day. Here is mine as an example.

When I wake up in the morning, I say to my higher power, "Thank you for the opportunity to experience a new day and all the possibilities it will bring, good or bad. Good is for my enjoyment, and whatever may seem bad is for my learning. I believe it's never the 'why,' but the 'what' that I need to learn from." Rather than "Why me?" Or "Why did they...?" I will ask, "What was my part? What could I have done differently? What do I do now?"

I meditate for five minutes, put in earplugs, and listen to my heartbeat. Your body noise amplifies when you plug your ears. It allows me to focus and not veer off with outside thoughts.

I wake up my son with a hug and say "I love you."

I do the mirror process, which consists of looking in the mirror and saying, "I see you, I hear you, and I love you."

Then I brush my teeth.

I read a daily inspirational passage while having Cuban coffee.

I make my bed and set the intention to have a human connection with someone and be open to learn.

I go to an Al-Anon meeting to keep my sanity and serenity.

I go to work.

I take ten minutes to stay still and do nothing in my car.

I exercise.

I eat dinner.

I journal, give thanks, and I always end my journal with, "I love me and l'il Garry." Then time to sleep.

Now, create a routine list that inspires you.

Remember to list as many routines as you can, and you can create more as you go along.

Routine List:

11. **FEAR LIST**—Familiarize yourself with your fears, get a piece of paper and write them down in a list. Then, next to each fear, label it as "survival" or "irrational." You will find that most of your fears are irrational. Don't let yourself get into a rut influenced by what-ifs. Get to know your fears and see what drives them.

12. **FUN LIST**- Keep a list of child-like things you can do. This is a list with no time frame, it serves as a reminder to achieve having fun. It also makes you accountable, so, there are no excuses. This will keep you out of your head and into fun.

13. **SUPPORT AND GUIDANCE LIST**—Make a support and guidance list on your device of three or more people you can call or text when you just need an ear to listen, or just to simply talk. Asking for help from the right people helps you build courage to deal with whatever is going on in your day or life. Have compassion and be available to receive a text or a call as well. Support and relationships are a two-way street.

First choice

Name: _____

Phone: _____

Second choice:

Name: _____

Phone: _____

Third choice

Name: _____

Phone: _____

Fourth choice

Name: _____

Phone: _____

ABOUT THE AUTHOR

I'm not a motivational speaker. I'm not against motivational speakers. They're great at getting you hyped up and focused, but that intensity for change tends to fade as you go back to your situational life and slip back into our old habits of self- criticism, self-doubt, and living without purpose. I'm going to give you something useful and more consistent: The Spiritual Compass. A guide that, no matter where you are in life, will give you direction and point you toward the best you. But, just like a regular compass, it can tell you where to go but it's up to you to put one foot in front of the other and do the work.

I'm Garry G and I've lived an unparalleled life that has led me to face many adversities. I've traveled to Japan, where I saw the ruins of the atomic bomb; to China, with its Great Wall and the Spring Temple Buddha that stands 597 feet high; and to South Africa for the World Cup, where I visited Robbins Island, where Nelson Mandela spent twenty-seven years in prison.

But my life was never easy. As a child I contemplated suicide because I couldn't believe how hard it was to be a kid. I was molested from seven to ten years old by a family friend. My parents were old-school disciplinarians, which as a kid felt abusive. I developed defense mechanisms to protect myself, which led me to become a bruiser who used violence to solve his problems. Due to fear and insecurity, I was lost, with no direction. The luckiest day of my life was meeting my mentor, who provided me the opportunity to experience nurture and unconditional love. That encounter not only changed my life, it actually saved my life.

Today I'm the trusted face for such companies as GEICO, Wells Fargo, Consumer Cellular, GoodRX, Avis, and many others, as well as a recognized mentor of major CEOs, Hollywood screenwriters, and well-known actors.

As I started to work on myself, the idea of the Spiritual Compass began to develop and I used it to guide me where I wanted to be. It led me to some amazing places, but even better, it gave me the tools I needed to help and inspire others.

For instance, I worked with a writer whose movies had grossed billions at the box office, but he hadn't worked in several years and felt he was finished in the industry. I urged him to use his talents to help others in his field and this revitalized his love of writing and his career. Once he chose a direction, it wasn't long until he landed major projects at Disney, Netflix, and more. As a bonus, he takes pride in knowing that the people he helped have started careers themselves in this highly competitive field.

Another woman was stuck in an abusive marriage. After she got out she felt she was left with nothing and she felt lost. I reminded her she was the mother of four children and had all the organization skills any company would want. Today she's the CEO of her own company.

In my time as a mentor, life coach, and a 12-step sponsor, I've had the pleasure to help dozens of people who have themselves gone on to sponsor and help countless others. As a speaker, I've been able to bring these tools to thousands of people, but I realized I could only affect lives in person, so I started to put these tried and true princi-ples down in a book. If you feel you don't have direction, if you feel lost, let the Spiritual Compass point you in the right direction.

It's always best to have a personal mentor. I recommend you seek one out, whether it be a therapist, a 12-step sponsor, or an emotionally healthy friend you can trust, but in the meantime, anyone can read or listen to a book. This is my gift to you, and I hope it changes your life the way it has changed mine.

GLOSSARY

Identity—This is who you are and the purpose of your existence, the part that the deity loved so much it had to create you. It is the critical element of consciousness, perfect and complete.

Self-Belief—This is the foundation of spiritual development. It gives you the willingness to take the risk to develop your identity. It is confidence based on observing your abilities and judgments.

Self-Acceptance— This can be described as the willingness to leave one's divine identity unaltered, and the decision to grow through one's developmental learning stages without self-criticism.

Self-Responsiveness—This is the acknowledgement of one's needs and positive self-care.

Self-Trust—This is the reliance on the integrity, strength, and ability of oneself.

Higher Power—This is any aspect of belief, which can provide an in-depth experience and have an internal and/or external spiritual consciousness.

Service—This is a form of giving to improve the life of others and oneself.

Surrender—This is the acknowledgment of an enforcing power greater than that of oneself; relieving self/ego from control of people, places, or things.

Willingness—This is the ability to take a positive approach to letting things happen on their own.

Truth—This is the self-evident manifestation of actuality and reality.

Love—A virtue of human kindness, compassion, interpersonal attraction, and emotion.

Action—Dynamics of energy, which creates movement.

Trust—This is the assured reliability of safety and honesty in a person or entity.

Compassion—This is a quantitative capability to hold and alleviate another's suffering.

Tolerance—This is the act of having the capacity to endure something that differs from yourself from an objective perspective.

Forgiveness—This is a genuine compassion for those who have wronged us, including ourselves, or where trust has been broken or lost.

Humility—This is the estimate of one's own importance and condition of being humble.

Perspective—This is having a meaningful interrelationship in the state of one's ideas.

Insight—This is the motivational awareness behind one's actions, thoughts, and self-knowledge.

Commitment—This is a pledge or promise, engaging oneself.

Joy—This is an emotion of deep happiness or satisfaction produced by something or someone greatly valued.

TESTIMONIALS

I met Garry in 2013, and instantly knew he would be my lighthouse to guide me in the right direction. Garry has an amazing spiritual insight, and has given me many tools to help me navigate through life.

Garry has the ability to help others tap into the deep and honest truth about themselves. He showed me how to go to the root of any issue in my life, and navigate through it towards a successful outcome.

My personal life and relationships have never been better! In addition, my professional career continues to excel. Garry is an amazing friend, mentor, and leader. I am thankful and grateful to have him in my life. I would not have the success in all of my relationships and career today if it were not for Garry and this book.

Andrew Compton, MBA

IF YOU PERSEVERE, STICK WITH IT,

you will have a real opportunity to achieve something.

Sure there will be storms along the way. And you

might not reach your goal right away. But if you do

your best and keep a true compass, you'll get there.

—Ted Kennedy